JOANNA MURRAY-SMITH's plays have been produced throughout Australia and all over the world, including *Honour*, which had a public reading with Meryl Streep and was produced on Broadway in 1998, the National Theatre, London, in 2003, and on the West End with Dame Diana Rigg in 2005. Other plays include *Three Little Words*; *L'Appartement*; *Fury*; *Songs for Nobodies*; *Switzerland*; *Pennsylvania Avenue*; *True Minds*; *Day One, A Hotel, Evening*; *Rockabye*; *Ninety*; *Bombshells*; *Rapture*; *Nightfall*; *Redemption*; *Love Child*; *Atlanta*; *Flame* and acclaimed adaptations of *Hedda Gabler* and *Scenes from a Marriage*, many of which have been translated into other languages. She has been nominated for and won many awards.

For Judy Kolt, with admiration and love.
And for my mother.

BERLIN

Joanna Murray-Smith

CURRENCY PRESS
The performing arts publisher

CURRENCY PLAYS

First published in 2021
by Currency Press Pty Ltd,
PO Box 2287, Strawberry Hills, NSW, 2012, Australia
enquiries@currency.com.au
www.currency.com.au

This revised edition first published in 2022

Reprinted 2023

Typeset by Currency Press.
Printed by CanPrint, Canberra, ACT.
Cover features Grace Cummings; photograph by Justin Ridler, courtesy of Melbourne Theatre Company.

Currency Press acknowledges the Traditional Owners of the Country on which we live and work. We pay our respects to all Aboriginal and Torres Strait Islander Elders, past and present.

NATIONAL LIBRARY OF AUSTRALIA

A catalogue record for this book is available from the National Library of Australia

Contents

ACKNOWLEDGEMENTS

Thanks go to Brett Sheehy and Melbourne Theatre Company and the supporters of the NEXT STAGE Writers' Program. Gratitude to the team of the first production, whose imprint is indelibly on this play forever. Thanks to Claire Grady for her patience and support. And as always to Raymond, Sam, Charlie and Lucie who were there with me in Berlin when *Berlin* first flickered into life.

JMS

Berlin was first produced by the Melbourne Theatre Company at the Sumner Theatre, Melbourne, on 22 April 2021, with the following cast:

CHARLOTTE	Grace Cummings
TOM	Michael Wahr

Director, Iain Sinclair
Set and Costume Designer, Christina Smith
Lighting Designer, Niklas Pajanti
Composer and Sound Designer, Kelly Ryall
Voice and Dialect Coach, Anna McCrossin-Owen
Assistant Director, Alastair Clark
Intimacy Coordinator, Michala Banas
Fight Choreographer, Lyndall Grant
Movement Consultant, Kirsty Reilly

Berlin was developed through Melbourne Theatre Company's NEXT STAGE program with the support of the MTC Playwrights Giving Circle Donors, The Ian Potter Foundation, Naomi Milgrom Foundation, The Myer Foundation, Malcolm Robertson Foundation and The University of Melbourne.

CHARACTERS

TOM, mid-20s, native English speaker, not German.

CHARLOTTE, mid-20s, beautiful, German.

SETTING

Spring. Now. A Berlin studio-loft. Antique furniture, found or inherited, supplemented by Ikea. Piles of books, pop culture bric-a-brac, maybe a fish tank, a chest of drawers, an old sofa. It has an idiosyncratic style and charm, elevated by large windows that overlook the street below. Offstage is a bedroom and a bathroom. Very out of place, looms a large eighteenth-century oil painting of a seascape with dramatic rain clouds in an ornate frame.

SCENE ONE

It's pitch black. Suddenly, the front door bursts open violently and two figures, locked together, stumble through the door. The energy of their locked bodies causes havoc in the space as they stumble chaotically, knocking over objects. It's impossible to know if their physicality is erotic or hostile. Are they making love or killing each other?

Something breaks.

They stop. In the darkness, CHARLOTTE *feels her way to a lamp and turns it on.*

Suddenly: TOM *and* CHARLOTTE *are standing in the low light, both early to mid-20s, both attractive, both a little drunk and breathless.*

They stare at each other as if sizing one another up, anew.

CHARLOTTE *picks up a packet of cigarettes and lights one as* TOM *watches her. She walks to the fridge, pulls out two bottles of beer, opens them and hands one to Tom.*

She puts a record on the record player, low.

She slinks down on the sofa. He follows her lead and sits opposite her.

There's debris on the coffee table from before she went out: bottles, jam jar glasses, chip packets. She's not much of a housekeeper.

CHARLOTTE: How did you know about the bar?
TOM: How did I know?
CHARLOTTE: How did you know about the bar?
TOM: The bar?
CHARLOTTE: Yes. [*Beat.*] How did you know about it?
TOM: Am I on trial?
CHARLOTTE: You might be.

Beat. Clearly extemporising for her amusement:

TOM: I got chatting to a German deejay.

She's going to catch him out:

CHARLOTTE: Where?
TOM: [*good job at nonchalant*] At … the gate lounge at Dubai.

CHARLOTTE: [*playing cynical*] *Was für einem Quatsch?*

TOM: I have a sixth sense when it comes to interesting people. It helped he had a tattoo on his neck …

CHARLOTTE: Of?

TOM: [*thinking fast*] A … kitten.

CHARLOTTE: What was his name?

Beat.

TOM: Kurt. 'Kurt, I said, I want the real Berlin. Not fucking Lonely Planet, fuck no. That's for loser American college grads trying to find a falafel. The *real* thing.' He demurred—

CHARLOTTE: I never learnt this verb.

TOM: I demur. You demur. He/she demurs … To back down.

CHARLOTTE: Okay.

TOM: He demurred: 'I don't know what the real Berlin is.' So I said: 'Well, let's start with a lively bar known for its beautiful, brainy female staff where I can have a stimulating conversation.'

CHARLOTTE: Of course you did!

TOM: Words to that effect. I bought him a beer for his trouble.

CHARLOTTE: There's no bar at a gate lounge.

TOM: [*delaying*] Of course there isn't! … Plane delayed.

Quick as a flash:

CHARLOTTE: Why?

TOM: [*even faster*] Geese.

Beat. Phew.

CHARLOTTE: *Geese?*

TOM: Geese, as it turns out, are a bigger threat than terrorists. Terrorists are a nuisance but they don't get sucked into our jet engines, alas.

CHARLOTTE: So …

TOM: While we waited for the geese to depart, they let us leave the gate lounge.

CHARLOTTE: *Geil!* [Great!]

TOM: And at one of those fake Irish pubs they have in airports called something like O'Hoolihans, he gave me the scoop on the secret Berlin doorway under the railway station and all that. Said it was the best bar in the city.

CHARLOTTE: Okay.

TOM: I arrived in Berlin. Attempted to check in to the hostel, only to discover a problem with my booking due to a Norwegian basketball team. They were full tonight. Briefly panicked, a passing nod to the tall Norwegians discussing clubs, went out with hope in my heart, bought my U-ticket at the *Buhnhof* with a lot of difficulty—

CHARLOTTE: You mentioned already—

TOM: Checked out some 'must sees' until dark. And then, summoning Kurt's instructions which I had indelibly written on my inner cortex, vortex, whatever, found the bar and there I was.

CHARLOTTE: Well, that's an answer.

TOM: And there you were. Good old Kurt came through and I had a lot of geese to thank.

She has a drink. No rush.

CHARLOTTE: I might have bought that. If it weren't for the part about looking for 'stimulating conversation'.

TOM: Well, you're wrong there. That definitely was said.

CHARLOTTE: *Du hast gehofft* Sex *zu haben!*

TOM: [*clearly disingenuous*] God no! *Last* thing on my mind. It was more your existential pow-wow I was after.

CHARLOTTE: You must feel cheated.

TOM: This *is* an existential pow-wow where I come from. You're a much more challenging sparring partner than Mum. Good old Mum. Love her, obviously, but you know, she could give a Ted-talk on folding tea-towels.

She laughs.

CHARLOTTE: Tell me the truth, *stranger*.

TOM: The truth?

CHARLOTTE: Give it to me straight.

TOM: The truth is … [*Beat.*] You fetchingly fetched me a beer and I noticed that you were extremely beautiful and I had to chat you up.

CHARLOTTE: I never learnt that verb.

TOM: I chat you up. You are chatted up. He/she chat, then go up to her apartment.

CHARLOTTE: He flirts. She demurs.

TOM: Fast learner.

Beat. They look at each other: undeniable attraction.

CHARLOTTE: Another beer? Schnapps?

TOM: Schnapps. Yes. Thank you.

She hands him one.

CHARLOTTE: You'd never make a spy.

TOM: Well, that's funny because as it happens, I *am* a spy.

CHARLOTTE: There you go again. *Schwindler.*

TOM: You're my dangerous mission.

She gets up and goes to a drawer and pulls out a joint, lights it and takes a hit.

She smokes it for a bit as they talk:

CHARLOTTE: Are you an agent or a double agent?

TOM: Do you think you can 'turn' me?

CHARLOTTE: I *know* I can …

Now he laughs. They stare at each other. Sexual tension.

TOM: I'm actually in industrial espionage. If I tell you …

CHARLOTTE: My lips are sealed—

TOM: I work for a company back home that's trying to get the inside edge on its competitor—

CHARLOTTE: That's why you're in Berlin?

Is he the real deal?

TOM: Of course, cyber espionage uses technology these days—iSherlock, obviously—but my company still believes it's hard to beat a man on the ground. Even if he's in a bar.

CHARLOTTE: Which industry?

TOM: *Lederhosen.*

She laughs. He laughs. He had her going there.

CHARLOTTE: Fuck you, arsehole.

TOM: I'm surprised you didn't smell a rat on iSherlock, frankly.

They drink, a beat. She passes him the joint.

CHARLOTTE: It's just … one night.

TOM: I know that.

CHARLOTTE: The sofa.

TOM: Of course the sofa.

CHARLOTTE: I'm not just some available sexual parts for capitalising.

TOM: That's very bad English.

CHARLOTTE: What should I say?

TOM: 'I'm not just some serendipitous pick-up at your erotic disposal.'

CHARLOTTE: And you'd say:

TOM: 'Of course not. Good God. As if.'

Stare at each other: are they giving each other signs?

CHARLOTTE: I was going to offer to show you around tomorrow. But I suppose if you're in espionage you don't need a tour guide?

TOM: Actually, with the budgets these days, they just send you off with some Novichok and Tripadvisor. I'd love a tour guide.

CHARLOTTE: [*slightly flirtatious*] Well … we'll see.

TOM: Cool … Of course, I've seen *some* edited highlights already … Nefertiti. The *Reichstag*. The Jewish Memorial full of Japanese girls in Hello Kitty onesies taking selfies … At which point, I was overwhelmed by an unstoppable realisation that humanity is doomed. So, I popped into the Ramones Museum. Fuck, that place must do well! One museum in a hundred monuments to grief that's just about great music.

CHARLOTTE: My mum saw them live here in '78.

TOM: That's sick.

CHARLOTTE: I've got all her vinyl. First release Stones. Joni Mitchell. Dylan. The parents are all into Spotify and the kids are into records.

TOM: Exactly. [*Indicating*] Is that your guitar?

CHARLOTTE: I play a bit. I write songs sometimes.

TOM: Play me something.

CHARLOTTE: Oh, I only do that for people I like.

He smiles.

So after the Ramones museum?

TOM: I needed a drink. Before I knew it, I was in your secret bar under the railway station, ordering a *Paulaner Salvator Doppel Bock*. Is that a shit name for a beer, or what? Anyway. You were slightly chilly delivering the beer, no doubt thinking: 'Fucking tourist', and I said something remarkable, witty and original:

CHARLOTTE: *Hello.*

TOM: Great recall. And tried in vain to start a conversation.

CHARLOTTE: I was working.

TOM: I think I asked you a question pulsating with significance.

CHARLOTTE: *Where is the men's room?*

TOM: And then I took a deep breath and said:

CHARLOTTE: 'You don't know any cheap hotels near here do you?' And I said: 'Are you homeless?' And you said:

TOM: 'God no. I have the Royal suite at the Adlon Kempinski but I need to shoot a music video tonight for Nick Cave.' Then, if I'm not mistaken, the tiniest promise of a smile, a slight softening, a bit more of 'Fucking tourists but this one's not completely awful …' And then. Well. I told you my African guy story which went nowhere. You were busy. As you said. So I left. And there I was, in the cold air, about to cross the street, filled with existential anxiety and—you could have blown me down—

CHARLOTTE: I never do this with a stranger!

TOM: [*beat as he realises …*] Of course, you wouldn't. You'd slipped out of the bar, through the punters and the drizzle to find me. Is there anything sadder than a foreigner standing alone in the damp dark with no place to go? Spontaneously, I turned around. You were there. In a puddle of lamplight looking very *The Third Man.*

CHARLOTTE: Vienna—

TOM: Waving.

CHARLOTTE: Uncertainly.

TOM: *Reprieve*, I thought.

CHARLOTTE: *On the verge of regret*, I felt.

I thought I'd been a bit unfriendly. You with your booked out hostel sob-story.

TOM: And you with your cushy inner-city loft space.

CHARLOTTE: I felt a bit bad as you headed for the exit.

TOM: I was bravely nursing the rejection as I left.

CHARLOTTE: I started thinking about national public relations. How I ought to be nice to a tourist so the word doesn't get around that we're stand-offish, or something. Thought I should extend the hand of global friendship.

TOM: *I'm leaving*, I thought. *I know when I'm pushing my luck.*

CHARLOTTE: *He's leaving*, I thought. *And maybe I don't want him to.*

TOM: *You blew it*, I thought to myself. *You with your boring story about the African guy at security and the Tic Tacs.*

CHARLOTTE: *He's all by himself*, I thought, *nowhere to stay and his Tic Tacs story was quite funny.*

TOM: *Shit story! Couldn't you do better than that, man?*

CHARLOTTE: *Really quite funny story that made me laugh out loud, if only for a moment.*

TOM: *That girl was adorable*, thought I.

Beat.

CHARLOTTE: *That boy was quite cute*, I said to Monika.

Beat.

TOM: And my heart started beating very loudly. Like a travel clock at Epidaurus.

CHARLOTTE: [*straight*] Really?

TOM: [*straight*] Didn't you hear it?

CHARLOTTE: Not over the band.

TOM: A *lot* fucking louder than the band and the band was loud.

CHARLOTTE: *Die Seidigenkettensagen.*

TOM: That would be German for really terrible, unbelievably shit music that belongs in someone's parents' Munich garage?

CHARLOTTE: They're very popular!

TOM: German pop … Your second biggest crime against humanity.

CHARLOTTE: [*hiding her amusement*] Fuck!

TOM: *Your face.*

CHARLOTTE: *That look.*

She moves closer to him. Is she going to touch him?

CHARLOTTE: So what you really wanted …

TOM: [*not moving towards her*] Mmm?

A moment ... is she going to kiss him? She gets closer.

CHARLOTTE: [*drawing nearer*] Let's not pretend.

He contemplates a kiss, then draws back.

TOM: You're right. *Refuge.*

CHARLOTTE: [*moving back in response*] I think you wanted something more than that.

TOM: I *did* want something more.

She raises her eyebrow, waiting. He moves in again.

Your sofa.

She moves in again.

CHARLOTTE: No-one ever wanted a sofa *more*.

Palpable sexual tension. She really wants him but he's slightly resistant. He's not making a move. She waits. For nothing. Stand off. She's puzzled and slightly miffed he's not jumping her. She lights a cigarette coolly.

So … Why are you in Berlin?

He looks at her, neutrally. She meets his gaze.

TOM: To find you.

CHARLOTTE: Seriously.

TOM: Seriously, to find you. I did my research. Tracked you down and *voilà*.

CHARLOTTE: Now you're just being creepy.

TOM: I dropped out of law. I pondered where I could find the meaning of life. And now I'm in Berlin looking for it.

CHARLOTTE: Nice story … I think …

TOM: What? … Say it.

CHARLOTTE: I think what you're looking for is sex, mister.

He takes a beat. Then CHARLOTTE *raises her dress provocatively and does a little sexy dance.*

TOM: [*relieved*] Well … men don't say no to sex, do they? In general. Regardless of what's on offer.

CHARLOTTE: I'm feeling so special.

TOM: No—I mean—Fuck.

CHARLOTTE: It's okay.

TOM: Forget that. I'm actually very choosy.

CHARLOTTE: [*teasing*] You mean, women don't like you?

TOM: Are you kidding? They *love* me.

She laughs. They stare at each other. They draw nearer. It seems certain to end in their lips touching but at the last moment, he breaks it.

Again, she's puzzled. What's he playing at?

Can I have another beer?

CHARLOTTE: Help yourself.

He goes to the makeshift kitchen, opens the fridge and pulls out two more beers which he opens. TOM *notices the painting.*

TOM: That's some painting!

CHARLOTTE: It *is*.

TOM: And if you don't mind me saying so, slightly incongruous.

CHARLOTTE: It's a Constable.

TOM: Well, well, an actual Constable.

CHARLOTTE: You have no idea who Constable is, do you?

TOM: [*appearing to bluff*] That's a bit insulting.

CHARLOTTE: He's a very famous artist.

TOM: I knew that. The old Constable. The famous artist.

CHARLOTTE: It's a good fake.

TOM: Obviously. Any fool can see that.

She laughs at his pretence.

CHARLOTTE: My mother thought it would cheer the place up.

TOM: It doesn't.

CHARLOTTE: I know … She's an artist.

TOM: For an artist, I'm not sure her instinct is top-notch.

CHARLOTTE: I don't want to hurt her feelings. Are you into art?

TOM: It's a personal obsession.

She smiles. TOM *brings the beers back, hands her one and raises his own: cheers. They drink.*

I must say, that's one of the things you do well. You make a good beer. And cars.

CHARLOTTE: Actually, also other things.

TOM: Do you think it's true that Germans don't have a sense of humour?

CHARLOTTE: I'm joking.

She laughs. He smiles.

It's all about the placement of the verb.

TOM: I have no idea at all what that means.

CHARLOTTE: German humour. The verb at the end comes. Which it the punchline ruins.

TOM: It's nice of you to let me hang out.

CHARLOTTE: You have a trustworthy face.

TOM: For real?

CHARLOTTE: I'm a good judge of faces.

TOM: Well, I'm not a serial killer.

As she speaks, she goes to withdraw a big kitchen knife from the knife block and holds it, for dramatic effect.

CHARLOTTE: That's what a serial killer would say though, isn't it? And then I'll be in my bedroom and I'll see the moonlit door-handle slowly turn and I'll know you're on the other side of the door with a great big kitchen knife and I'll reach for my phone and it will be out of battery and my heart will be beating like—like a travel clock at Epidaurus—and I'll know in hours the place will be crawling with forensic cops analysing blood spatters.

TOM: You're cute. And imaginative. And really beautiful.

She thrusts the knife into the wooden bench.

CHARLOTTE: All that and great in bed.

Eye contact. Beat.

TOM: I believe it.

Beat as they have a stand off. A slight physical dance between them: one step closer, one back, a misread. The awkwardness broken:

This is a very cool place. How long have you been here?

She's still puzzling over why he's not jumping her, but going along ...

CHARLOTTE: Four years. Before *Prenzlauer Berg* became a Mecca for cashed up hipsters in beanies. The only downside is Heinz, my alt-right neighbour.

TOM: Does he desecrate graves?

CHARLOTTE: Worse. He drops in with left-over pasta and then starts lecturing me on how Jews and Turks are taking over the world.

TOM: Are you an heiress or something?

CHARLOTTE: Oh, *Scheiss*! I've been trying to keep it quiet! Pharmaceuticals.

TOM: I do love a pharmaceutical heiress. They're the best kind.

CHARLOTTE: Hence the Bavarian castle.

TOM: *Scheiss*! A Bavarian castle! Where?

CHARLOTTE: Bavaria.

TOM: [*saving himself*] Obviously but north, south, east, west?

CHARLOTTE: A little bit of all of them. It's a big castle.

TOM: I thought so! It's that look of entitlement you have.

CHARLOTTE: … Actually my father did buy this for me. Out of guilt. And because I'm studying. Which is *why* I'm studying. I just want to write but my father thinks that's delusional.

TOM: Are they here in Berlin, your folks?

CHARLOTTE: They separated when I was seven, hence the guilt. He's an immature hedonist hedge fund guy who lives in London. He works for *Deutsches Bank* turning money into money. My mother lives in Berne with her shrink boyfriend. She's a narcissistic sculptor. See that?

She points out an unattractive brass sculpture.

TOM: … Oh.

CHARLOTTE: I know. What do you think it is?

TOM: … An ovary?

She laughs.

CHARLOTTE: It's a cat.

TOM: Fuck.

CHARLOTTE: That's not one of her best.

TOM: I believe you! You're very objective about your parents.

CHARLOTTE: Most of my life is spent trying not to turn into them.

TOM: Your kids will say the same thing about you.

CHARLOTTE: Are you kidding? I'm the one who disrupts the gene pool. If I thought I'd become my parents … Christ … I'd shoot myself. Genetic inheritance is such a depressing concept.

TOM: Isn't it? I only believe in it because my parents do.

She smiles.

CHARLOTTE: Hey there.

TOM: Hey there …

Beat. He takes her hand and pulls her towards him. They're standing very close to each other. They look into each other's face.

Kiss me.

CHARLOTTE: You've changed your tune.

TOM: Kiss me.

CHARLOTTE: No.

TOM: You've changed your tune.

CHARLOTTE: [*playfully*] You had your chance.

TOM: Just one. We'll leave it there.

CHARLOTTE: Leave what there?

TOM: The kiss. One kiss. And after that, we'll have the memory as a souvenir.

CHARLOTTE: A souvenir of—?

TOM: This. Now. A really interesting night at the very least.

CHARLOTTE: No.

Beat. He looks out at the dark, through the big windows. A puddle of street-light illuminates the pavement.

TOM: What are the shining things? In the pavement down there? Those little brass squares? I've seen them everywhere.

CHARLOTTE: The *stolpersteine*. 'Stumbling blocks.' They're memory sites.

TOM: What does that mean?

CHARLOTTE: There are thousands of them, all over the city. There are three outside this building.

TOM: Stumbling blocks?

CHARLOTTE: An artist made them. Symbolic memorials. '*Hier wohnte* … Here lived … Esther Rosen. Born 1927, deported June seventh 1939, murdered Auschwitz 1942.'

TOM: Who was Esther Rosen?

CHARLOTTE: A girl who lived in this building. The artist found the last chosen residence of people who were murdered by the Nazis. He thought the big fascistic type memorials were too easy to avoid, whereas these little inscribed plaques are a part of everyday life. So he just keeps making them.

TOM: Fuck. That's brilliant.

CHARLOTTE: There used to be a saying, you know, by anti-semites—when they stumbled: 'A Jew must be buried here'.

TOM: Charming.

CHARLOTTE: So Demnig—the artist—has kind of reclaimed that ironically. Some people don't like that we're stepping on the dead.

TOM: What do you think?

CHARLOTTE: I think that the artist touching each one … reinstates life to the person he's remembering. They're little stars of memory in our daily commutes.

She pours them wine. He lifts his glass.

TOM: [*toasting*] To little stars.

CHARLOTTE: My stepfather brought this. He's a wine snob so I'm hoping it's good. He does this.

She picks up the glass, swirls it, sniffs it, holds it up to the light.

TOM: Oh, I love the glass swivel …

He does it convincingly and sniffs.

Hmm … Quite a lot of blackcurrant. Maybe … the *Rheingau* … a *Spatburgunder* … that hint of grass …

CHARLOTTE: It's Australian.

TOM: You should know I'm only twenty percent authentic. The rest is pure strategy.

CHARLOTTE: And which part is speaking now?

TOM: You might be too clever for me.

CHARLOTTE: *Might* be?

Beat. They sip in silence.

TOM: Favourite poem?

CHARLOTTE: Rilke of course. 'I am much too alone in this world, yet not alone enough.'

TOM: Read it to me.

CHARLOTTE: I don't need to read it. I carry it inside me.

TOM: So tell it to me.

CHARLOTTE: No.

TOM: Why not?

CHARLOTTE: It's too … I can't do that. It would be like … licking your body. It would be like … sleeping curled up inside you. It would be like … sharing a peach.

This feels like enticement ... seduction ... but he's afraid.

TOM: Are you published?

CHARLOTTE: Of course I'm published! God!

TOM: Yeah?

CHARLOTTE: Yeah!

Beat.

[*Mustering the confession*] In obscure but important journals.

TOM: That's impressive. At your age.

CHARLOTTE: You sound like my uncle.

TOM: No, it's just—I've got nothing to show for twenty-four years on the planet. Three under-fifteen tennis trophies and a bronze surf-life-saving certificate and an incomplete law degree.

CHARLOTTE: I don't want to waste time.

TOM: Isn't that the major qualification for being a poet? Studying autumn leaves. Smelling babies' heads?

She laughs.

CHARLOTTE: No. The major qualification is talent.

TOM: With which you overflow.

CHARLOTTE: Obviously! When I win the Nobel, you'll say 'I slept on her sofa'.

TOM: An ambitious poet?

CHARLOTTE: Absolutely … contrary to reputation, we're all ruthless ambition and *schadenfreude*.

TOM: I can tell you're good.

CHARLOTTE: If you can tell me why I'm a good poet without reading the poetry, I'll kiss you.

Beat. They meet each other's eyes for the challenge. TOM *thinks.*

TOM: You know how to build expectation …

She's impressed. But he's not done.

You use language enigmatically and—

CHARLOTTE: And?

TOM: You're great in bed. Just like Emily Dickinson.

She laughs.

Well?

He looks at her. She's so cool.

CHARLOTTE: I didn't say when.

TOM: No, you're right. We should keep this simple. Stick to the plan.

CHARLOTTE: A few beers, a place to sleep.

TOM: Existential chit-chat.

CHARLOTTE: Then—*auf wiedersehen.*

TOM: Forever. Alone but not alone enough.

She doesn't want to be keener than he is but she is keen. He eyes a photo of two kids.

You're cute. Is that your brother?

CHARLOTTE: Yes. He's dead.

TOM: Shit!

CHARLOTTE: Chased a ball onto the street. Hit by a car. He was four. I was six.

TOM: [*shocked*] That's a sad story, Charlotte.

CHARLOTTE: We all have a sad story though, don't we, Tom?

TOM: Do we?

CHARLOTTE: I ended up going back and forth to each parent—London, Berlin. Not because they couldn't live without me but because they couldn't stand … the idea of relinquishing anything to the other.

TOM: Why do people always split in the face of disaster? Wouldn't suffering make everyone else seem infuriatingly innocent? Only *your* parents knew what it was to lose *their* kid. Doesn't that bind them forever?

CHARLOTTE: No. Because—

She stops.

TOM: What?

CHARLOTTE: Well … Love is an act of hope.

TOM: Is it?

CHARLOTTE: Two people agree to hope against the odds.

Beat. He's completely tripped up by her. She's absolutely special. He wants her but knows he can't have her.

CHARLOTTE: It is a *verschwörung* … a—

She tries to remember the word.

CHARLOTTE / TOM: [*together*] *Conspiracy.*

CHARLOTTE: A conspiracy to throw cynicism out of the window. I suppose they made that once, that pact. But then when Daniel died … well, you can't wind back to innocence, can you? Innocence is something you only ever have once.

TOM: I don't remember innocence.

CHARLOTTE: There's *your* sad story.

TOM: Do you miss him?

CHARLOTTE: I don't know. Sometimes I think he's here.

TOM: Where?

CHARLOTTE: Downstairs. Where all brothers should be. Alive but not present. In the vicinity but not cramping my style. He's not dead. He's just downstairs.

He studies her. He moves towards her. He's very close to her face. He wants her to bend to his mouth but she doesn't: she's willing herself to stay cool. He realises she's not going to kiss him and draws back. He lifts his glass.

TOM: *Prost.*

She lifts hers.

CHARLOTTE: *Prost.*

They drink.

Fair trade.

TOM: [*catching on*] What do you want to know?

CHARLOTTE: Favourite book?

TOM: *Tintin and the Red Sea Sharks*.

CHARLOTTE: But he's such an exemplar of racist colonialism!

TOM: Is that why you want to be a poet? So you can wield your superior world view?

CHARLOTTE: Is that why you studied law? So you can wield your superior world view? Favourite food?

TOM: Schnitzel.

CHARLOTTE: Favourite band?

TOM: The Ramones.

CHARLOTTE: What do you want out of life?

TOM: You to recite the Rilke poem.

CHARLOTTE: Girlfriend?

TOM: Broke up in October. Boyfriend?

CHARLOTTE: I dated a professional footballer for three months last year.

TOM: Is that it, then? The questions?

CHARLOTTE: *Why Berlin*?

Beat.

TOM: Vague family connection.

CHARLOTTE: [*surprised*] You're German?

TOM: My great-grandfather lived on *Drakestrasse*.

CHARLOTTE: Wow! You hold your cards close to your ribs.

He smiles to himself.

Drakestrasse! Near the embassies?

TOM: Yes.

CHARLOTTE: I go for long walks near there, in the *Tiergarten*, writing poems in my head. And when I'm rich I go to Cafe Einstein for *Hausgebeizter Lachs mit Kren*.

TOM: I actually went to find the house yesterday.

CHARLOTTE: Was it there?

TOM: The building's still there. But it's an architectural office.

CHARLOTTE: Cool it's still there.

TOM: It is cool. But I had a fantasy I'd look in the window and it would *all* still be there: his library. And art. Antiquities … The small marble nude Aphrodite looking as if she was surprised by someone on her way to take a bath …

CHARLOTTE: What happened to him?

Beat?

TOM: He died at Bergen Belsen.

CHARLOTTE: [*excited*] Oh fuck, *you're Jewish*!

TOM: [*ironically upbeat*] Oh fuck, *I know*!

CHARLOTTE: That's so *great*!

He's astonished by this reaction.

TOM: It is?

CHARLOTTE: You know … I could tell!

He regards her, hint of a raised eyebrow.

Your air of intellectual … intensity.

Is she serious? She takes in his sardonic expression.

It's a compliment!

TOM: Okay, but to be honest, I'm not super Jewish.

CHARLOTTE: What does this mean?

TOM: I'm mainly Jewish when in the company of anti-semites.

She takes this on the chin.

CHARLOTTE: Oh fuck, did I offend you, Tom?

TOM: I'm not angry, I'm just disappointed.

She relaxes as she sees his smile.

CHARLOTTE: I get this. It's what the parents say to the naughty children.

TOM: Don't worry, your face buys you instant indemnity.

CHARLOTTE: And your father's side?

TOM: Super-Wasp as in Christmas trees in every room and an allergy to hugging.

CHARLOTTE: Okay.

TOM: You didn't say *that* was great.

CHARLOTTE: I *did* offend you.

TOM: I'm a bit of a stickler for equal opportunity condescension.

CHARLOTTE: Okay, so—Tell me the story.

TOM: The whole story?

CHARLOTTE: [*playing*] The *whole* story, you big Jew!

He laughs.

TOM: My grandmother Rosa and her sister Elsa were the daughters of Jules. They survived the war by being hidden by nice nuns in a convent.

CHARLOTTE: I didn't know there were nice nuns.

TOM: Turns out that prior to whipping small children at school in the seventies and skating over institutionalised paedophilia, there were some very nice nuns.

CHARLOTTE: What happened to Rosa and Elsa?

TOM: When I was seven I asked my mother why I didn't have a grandmother. She told me that after she was born, her mother walked into a lake and drowned herself.

CHARLOTTE: God! She told you that? At seven?

TOM: Just like that.

CHARLOTTE: Why?

TOM: Because she was envious and resentful. That I was innocent. I had something she could never have again. So she confiscated it. *Let me tell you a bedtime story about six million Jews and then you'll understand what* my *life's been like!*

Beat.

CHARLOTTE: That's … angry of you.

TOM: I'm an angry person.

Beat. She picks up the subtle seriousness of this.

CHARLOTTE: So is … Is any family left in Europe?

TOM: Some distant cousin in Vienna. I thought of going but I'm told the place is crawling with neo-Nazis and dancing ponies.

CHARLOTTE: So you came to Berlin even though there's no-one left?

TOM: The family connection seemed like a reason for Berlin. And I ended up with some money.

CHARLOTTE: How?

Beat. He's slightly reluctant.

TOM: It was just a little … windfall.

She doesn't know the word. Explaining:

From the heavens.

CHARLOTTE: [*getting it*] *Pfennige vom Himmel*. Where from?

Beat.

TOM: I was in a car crash.

CHARLOTTE: *Das ist shrecklich!*

TOM: There was a court case. I got some money.

CHARLOTTE: Were you hurt?

TOM: Crushed vertebrae. Crushed youthful effervescence. Dead friend.

CHARLOTTE: [*shocked*] Fuck … That's terrible!

TOM: Especially for him.

CHARLOTTE: God … Oh my God, Tom … I'm so sorry.

TOM: It was a while ago and … You weren't driving.

CHARLOTTE: Were you?

TOM: No.

Beat.

CHARLOTTE: *Also was ist passiert?*

He overcomes his reluctance, but it's still there.

TOM: We were hitch-hiking to a friend's place in the country. Summer rain. It was wet and the driver ran off the road … and hit a tree.

CHARLOTTE: Fucking hell! *Das ist verrukt* ... [*She takes it in*] You don't have to talk about this if you don't want to.

TOM: Okay.

Beat. She's consumed by his story.

CHARLOTTE: You must have thought … what if the driver never stopped for us?

TOM: I thought I didn't have to talk about it?

CHARLOTTE: Shit. Sorry.

She studies him. He takes a moment.

TOM: She passed us. One boy with a red backpack, one boy in a blue rain jacket. Then she felt bad … leaving us in the rain, two kids … So she made a U-turn and came back to get us … And sixty Ks down the wet road, the car skidded and hit a tree. The boy with the red backpack was killed instantly.

She's really affected by this.

CHARLOTTE: You must remember his name.

TOM: I do.

Beat.

CHARLOTTE: How do you make sense of that?

TOM: Shit happens.

CHARLOTTE: Fuck no, Tom, please.

TOM: Okay … 'Really bad things frequently occur without apparent reason and ruin everything forever.'

CHARLOTTE: Did you ever meet the driver again?

TOM: The killer?

CHARLOTTE: 'Killer' is a bit cruel. Was she drunk?

TOM: No.

CHARLOTTE: She was just driving down a highway. She was in the wrong place at the wrong time. The rain. The road. Unchosen circumstances waiting for a … protagonist. Like the driver who hit my brother.

TOM: At the inquest. She told me she couldn't be morally responsible for events that weren't in her control.

CHARLOTTE: Well … She's right.

TOM: I told her that people could be responsible for a death without being guilty of it.

CHARLOTTE: That's … brutal.

She looks at him, reassessing something.

TOM: A kid chases a ball and dies. Two friends stand on the side of a highway and one dies. The drivers didn't make those things happen. But they still happened because of *them*. Where does that leave our moral judgement?

CHARLOTTE: I don't judge the man who hit my brother. It could have happened to any of us.

TOM: He was driving too fast. He reacted too slowly.

CHARLOTTE: I don't judge him. I swear.

TOM: Forgiveness is a construct. Maybe a useful one, but mostly inauthentic. At least at a molecular level. You are judging even when you think you're not. You might pay yourself the compliment of forgiveness but deep down, you're in a state of rage.

CHARLOTTE: That's a very arrogant assumption.

TOM: I think it's arrogant to assume you don't. Why *wouldn't* blame exist? The pain does! Why wouldn't the rage? And that rage directs your life with stealthy determination.

CHARLOTTE: What does that mean?

TOM: We try to fix our past. Consciously or unconsciously. Over and over again. Attempting to rewrite history.

CHARLOTTE: How did I 'fix' my brother's death?

Beat.

TOM: You don't know?

CHARLOTTE: No.

Beat.

TOM: You rescue people.

CHARLOTTE: *What* people?

TOM: You rescued *me*.

CHARLOTTE: What?

Beat.

TOM: I left you. Like he did. And you came for me.

CHARLOTTE: What?

TOM: I walked out of the club. I was about to cross the street. You looked up and saw me. And you waved to come back.

CHARLOTTE: I—?

TOM: Waved to your brother.

Beat.

You were bringing him back. From the brink. Only it was me.

CHARLOTTE: You think I'm driven to save young men?

TOM: Shit yes, I do.

CHARLOTTE: That's complete and utter rubbish, Tom. That's just amateur psychobabble.

TOM: There's this guy called Nagel—a philosopher—he says everything we do basically 'belongs to a world that we have not created'. Our actions are made up of luck—the chance elements that compose our character and therefore our choices and therefore our actions. If a murderer's context and history and upbringing and circumstances create him, then can we blame him for the act of murder?

CHARLOTTE: You're talking about free will?

TOM: Was your brother's death—was my friend's death—anyone's fault?

CHARLOTTE: Okay, we are driven by subterranean impulses, but we can interrupt them. We can refuse them. Otherwise, we would never hold anyone accountable for anything.

TOM: So your brother's death might have been interrupted. If the driver thought to himself, 'I'm speeding and I might kill someone'.

CHARLOTTE: Yes.

TOM: But what if he was incapable of that thought because of who he was and all the circumstances of his being?

CHARLOTTE: I don't believe that.

Beat.

TOM: Neither do I. But there's no doubt that we are compelled by forces we don't understand. History and place and time … I am here because of those things, even though I feel as if I'm here for no other reason than … I'm excited by you.

Beat.

CHARLOTTE: And I'm … excited by you.

Beat.

TOM: But that's not the only reason why you invited me.
CHARLOTTE: So why did you come and why did I invite you?
TOM: …Let's find out.

Beat.

CHARLOTTE: And what happened to the boy in the blue rain jacket? After the accident?
TOM: You tell me.

She looks at him. It's a moment of intense intimacy after sharing their sad stories. Does she dare?

CHARLOTTE: His youth ended … He became obsessed by his own mortality … He took drugs and drank too much … He dropped out of school … He looked to his history to make sense of things … He came to Berlin … He met Charlotte, a waitress in a bar … He left the bar and suddenly, driven by unconscious forces to do with her dead brother, she stopped him … She offered him a place to stay … they drank a lot … and for the first time ever he told the truth about what he'd been through.

She's right. Long beat.

TOM: And then?

They stare at each other a moment. She recites the Rilke.

CHARLOTTE: 'I want to mirror your image to its fullest perfection,
never be blind or too old
to uphold your weighty wavering reflection.
I want to unfold.
Nowhere I wish to stay crooked, bent;

for there I would be dishonest, untrue.
I want my conscience to be
true before you;
want to describe myself like a picture I observed
for a long time, one close up,
like a new word I learned and embraced,
like the everday jug,
like my mother's face,
like a ship that carried me along
through the deadliest storm.'

Beat. He's entranced.

TOM: 'I want my conscience to be true before you,' she says.
CHARLOTTE: She does.

He moves closer to her.

TOM: Your footballer isn't going to come bursting in here, is he? Primed to beat me to a pulp?
CHARLOTTE: Why would he do that?
TOM: For kissing his ex.
CHARLOTTE: Are you, Tom?
TOM: I am, Charlotte.

Long beat. He looks at her. His expression is anxious, even reluctant. But he can't resist. He kisses her. She lets him. They curl into each other, passionately awakened.

Lights down.

SCENE TWO

---

4 a.m. The loft is in darkness. TOM, *bare-chested, stands at the doorway from the bedroom. Moonlight partially illuminates the painting. He stares at it.*

The moment breaks. Hungover, he pours a glass of water and drinks it down fast. He picks up his phone and checks his messages. He glances at the bedroom door, which is almost closed. He dials.

TOM: [*quietly, into phone*] Hey … Yes, I'm here … Yes, it is. Yes, I'm sure. Where are you?

He walks over to the window and looks out on the deserted street, left, right, and then sights what he's looking for.

Something's happened … I can't explain now. It's going to take longer … Don't call. Don't wait … I'll call you.

He hangs up, looks back out.

CHARLOTTE, *very sexy in Tom's over-sized shirt, enters silently and watches him.*

She comes over to him at the window, surprising him. He quickly slips the phone in his pocket, assuming she didn't see or hear.

Did I wake you?

CHARLOTTE: No. I'm a bad sleeper. I'm too excited about the next day. I want to know what happens next.

He stares at this incredible woman. Everything she says excites him.

TOM: *I* happen next.

She puts her arms around his neck. They kiss: the ardent aftermath of a passionate encounter.

CHARLOTTE *tries to go to the kitchen, but he pulls her back and kisses her again, with hunger.*

She pulls away gently.

CHARLOTTE: *Scheiss*! You make me dizzy … Tea?

TOM: *Bitte.*

She fills and puts the kettle on.

She prepares tea as TOM *continues looking out of the window.*

CHARLOTTE: I don't usually do that.

TOM: Offer tea?

CHARLOTTE: Sleep with a stranger

TOM: Well … thank you for acting out of character.

While the kettle boils, CHARLOTTE *picks up some of the empty bottles from earlier. He looks at her. A strange moment of anxiety or compunction in him. She notes it. Stares at him.*

I never intended for this.

She laughs.

CHARLOTTE: It's okay, Tom. I'm a grown up. I can take responsibility for my own—

Cutting in:

TOM: I really like you.

Beat. She looks at him curiously.

CHARLOTTE: I … really like you, too.

She's studying him, trying to decipher …

TOM: Everything has *...changed.*

CHARLOTTE: What does that mean?

TOM: [*struggling to explain*] Everything I wanted, everything I dreamt about before last night happened in a different universe. A universe in which ... I didn't know you.

CHARLOTTE: [*sardonic, puzzled*] Cool.

TOM: And now it's different. I am going to start again. From *now*. So—

CHARLOTTE: [*puzzled*] So?

TOM: Time, now, *this* world, begins now! Well … began at one a.m. when we walked through the door … That's when the clock started and we began.

CHARLOTTE: I don't understand anything you're saying! And I don't think it's the language barrier … You're suggesting something happened last night, something—

TOM: Fuck, yes! *Yes*!

She looks at him: he's not laughing.

CHARLOTTE: I think I'm maybe a little bit scared of you.

TOM: I'm scared of me, too. I have a tendency to ruin things.

CHARLOTTE: I have a tendency to save them. As you have pointed out.

TOM: So save them. Save *us*.

She looks at him. What does he mean?

CHARLOTTE: I don't even know your last name.

TOM: Claiborne. Thomas Jules Claiborne.

CHARLOTTE: Nice to meet you, Thomas Jules Claiborne. I'm Charlotte Greta Werner.

TOM: Hello Charlotte Greta Werner.

He glances at the painting, around the room, brain whirring. All soberness now suddenly dispelled. He's alive with a proposition.

TOM: [*sincere, smitten*] Let's fucking go!

CHARLOTTE: [*laughing*] Go where?

TOM: Anywhere!

CHARLOTTE: I don't even know who you are!

TOM: Fuck it, Charlotte. Let's just run!

CHARLOTTE: [*enjoying the fun*] I can't tell when you are serious! Are you serious?

TOM: Run with me, Charlotte. This is—I don't—I didn't—This—this is something—*wondrous*.

She realises that he is *serious.*

CHARLOTTE: Okay, Thomas Jules Claiborne. I—I also—last night was also, for me—

TOM: [*petrified, hopeful*] It was?

CHARLOTTE: Yes. It was. But … you know … .

TOM: What?!

CHARLOTTE: … Can we trust it?

TOM: Of course we can!

CHARLOTTE: We met in a fucking bar! We can't tell our kids we met in a bar! They'll know that I slept with random tourists!

TOM: No! It's romantic! That the—you know—forces aligned! I was in the bar. You were in the bar. And now we have little Freddie and Alice and, and, and Hedwig. That makes you magnificently spontaneous and heroically poetic.

CHARLOTTE: Not a slut?

TOM: An oracle!

CHARLOTTE: So it means something?

TOM: This—*this* is—*I'd wage my life on it*—*this* is to be trusted.

CHARLOTTE: Okay! But we don't have to leave Berlin! I want to take you places. We can go back to bed and then fuck and then sleep and then get coffee and cinnamon buns and tonight we'll go dancing to

Clarchens Ballhaus and I'll show you the room with mirrors, the old Berlin.

TOM: I don't want the old Berlin. I want the *new* Berlin! I've never—fuck! Let's forget everything that's behind us.

CHARLOTTE: *What* 'behind us'?

TOM: All of it! These … decrepit, fucked up legacies! All of it … the old buildings.

CHARLOTTE: The buildings?

TOM: Full of the myths of the past and the broken hearts and dirty little secrets!

CHARLOTTE: I'm dying to know your dirty little secrets!

TOM: Time began at one a.m. There *are* no secrets for Tom and Charlotte.

CHARLOTTE: Are you sure?

TOM: Because we have no past. No past. No secrets.

CHARLOTTE: [*casually*] So … who were you on the phone to?

Beat. TOM *is shocked she overheard.*

[*Casually*] Girlfriend? Boyfriend?

He's paralysed a moment.

It's okay. You don't have to explain.

She passes him his tea. His excitement has evaporated.

TOM: My brother.

Beat.

CHARLOTTE: You lucky thing.

Is he lying? If he's lying—why?

Where is he?

TOM: Downstairs.

CHARLOTTE: Funny.

TOM: I'm serious. About us. It's not rational but I'm sick of rational! *Something buried in us is doing the real stuff.* In some chemical fucking *rave*. Okay, Charlotte, think about it. But think fast.

They both sip, not breaking eye contact. In unison, they rest their mugs. She lights a cigarette. She sits on the sofa. He pulls himself together, calmer, sits beside her.

CHARLOTTE: 'There is a pain—so utter—It swallows substance up—Then covers the Abyss with Trance—So Memory can step Around—across—upon it.' Emily Dickinson.

He absorbs this a moment before she continues:

The pain was so utter, it swallowed up the substance between my parents. And I resolved that I wouldn't let *my* substance be swallowed by grief. His death was not my death. *Is* not my death.

I have spent a lot of time wondering if he was angry … that little kid. That moment. When he knew.

A moment. She's surprised herself.

I've never told anyone that.

TOM: [*reacting to the weird thought*] Jesus. Charlotte—

CHARLOTTE: Was he furious? Why shouldn't he be? Did he think, dying: [*Directly at Tom*] *Why me and why not her?* Didn't you think that? You must have. You must, sometimes, wonder if your friend, as he lay there—

TOM: [*interrupting, quietly*] I've wondered. Yes.

CHARLOTTE: Going over every detail …

TOM: If one thing had been different—If the rain had stopped. If she'd been three kilometres ahead.

CHARLOTTE: Just one, tiny thing. Bending down to tie a shoe lace.

TOM: And that same principle is true now. If I walk out now. If I choose to leave at five a.m., perhaps offended by your question or—or—frightened of something—and at the front door I decide to walk to clear my head—

CHARLOTTE: You forgot your brother, downstairs—

TOM: That's right! My brother, lingering by a tree out there on the street. So he walks with me, and as we're crossing Alexanderplatz at 5.33, we stop to buy coffee at a pop-up and a truck driven by a terrorist hurtles towards us across the square, crushing bollards, sending early morning commuters screaming, others film it, cops yell into walkie-talkies and it suddenly explodes, killing us. [*Beat.*] Yes. [*Beat.*] What if I didn't choose to walk? What if I left twenty minutes earlier? One detail might change the outcome either way.

He kisses her suddenly, briefly on the mouth.

The decision to kiss you goodbye saves me or kills me.

CHARLOTTE: I vote 'Save'.

He takes a moment.

TOM: After the accident … every instinct became an existential crisis … Who got into the back-seat first? *I* did. For a while, I obsessively noticed every tiny choice in case it made *the difference*. Every door I opened, every walk to the store … A left turn. A right turn. And coming here … was intended to be … a disrupter. To focus on a bigger story than … the incidental.

CHARLOTTE: What is that bigger story?

TOM: As it turns out. You. Me.

CHARLOTTE: Frightened of what?

TOM: Frightened?

CHARLOTTE: You said: 'If I choose to leave at five a.m, perhaps frightened of something … ' Frightened of what?

TOM: That I met a girl in a bar who ended up being my lodestar, who destroyed my autonomy, unravelled my intentions and made time start again.

She's taken by his seriousness.

CHARLOTTE: What is a 'lodestar'?

TOM: *You*.

CHARLOTTE: [*powerfully affected*] I've never met anyone like you.

TOM: [*softly*] So … we're leaving.

CHARLOTTE: For where?

TOM: Portugal. Samoa. Let's see the polar bears in Hudson Bay.

CHARLOTTE: But the geese!

TOM: I'll handle the geese! I have money. Let's just go. Leave this apartment. Leave the painting and your great-grandfather and your ex-boyfriend and your mother's cat sculpture. Let's leave Berlin. And we'll start again.

He takes her in his arms and they kiss again, passionately, in raptures. They stop, stare at each other.

TOM: This can't end now.

He starts to undress her. It's very sexy and tender. She allows him to.

TOM *grabs the petals from the flowers from the vase and throws them in the air and they land around and on her.*

She laughs.

He looks at her, ravishing on the sofa. The gaze itself is like sex.

'I want my conscience to be true before you …'

Beat. She looks at him, captivated.

He walks over to her record player and collection, pulls out a Ramones record and puts it on.

She meets his gaze.

[*Astonished at this*] I found you.

As the music starts, he pulls the naked [or semi-naked] CHARLOTTE *off the sofa and pulls her towards him and they start to dance manically, crazy, happy, funny, singing along to the lyrics of the Ramones 'I Wanna Be Sedated'.*

SCENE THREE

Morning. Sun streaming through the windows. TOM *squeezing juice.* CHARLOTTE *lying on the sofa with coffee.*

CHARLOTTE: So, Mr Claiborne, what happens now?

He brings her juice.

TOM: Now you get juice.

CHARLOTTE: Bigger picture.

TOM: Having triumphed through EU trade liberalisation, Germany will be badly impacted by Euro-scepticism. Russia collapses, China disintegrates into multiple mini Chinas, Poland gets cocky, the Far Right take over Britain and the US implodes in civil war. In a nutshell.

CHARLOTTE: Hmm … not that big.

He moves towards her, lifts her chin to kiss her. She kisses back.

You haven't lived till you've eaten a cinnamon bun from *Zeit fur Brot* on *Eberswalder Strasse.*

TOM: I know nothing excites a German more than a carbohydrate but I'm prepared to try.

CHARLOTTE: These are *better* than sex. Even with you.

TOM: Now I *know* you're lying.

She laughs.

CHARLOTTE: You've hardly seen anything of Berlin, *Mister*.

TOM: I've seen Nefertiti, *Miss*.

CHARLOTTE: Did you like Nefertiti's bust?

TOM: I think you mean the bust of Nefertiti … I liked. What the hell is she doing in Berlin, I'd like to know?

CHARLOTTE: We found her up in Egypt in 1913 and the Egyptians didn't want her.

TOM: You mean by the time the Egyptians realised she was treasure, she'd been taken hostage in Berlin. *Just like me.*

CHARLOTTE: [*playfully provocative*] Nothing wrong with opportunism.

TOM: To the victor the spoils?

CHARLOTTE *lifts her coffee cup in a toast.*

CHARLOTTE: To explorers, plunderers, romantics.

TOM: Where is your shame?

She laughs. Gets up, starts making a new plunger of coffee.

CHARLOTTE: I'm unusual. Germans are so fucking tortured!

TOM: [*jokey*] Well … surely a little bit of shame … .?

CHARLOTTE: Fuck no, we've been sitting it out long enough! It's time to dance!

TOM: Really?

CHARLOTTE: We're so keen to demonstrate we're not recklessly nationalistic, we've forgotten who we are. The good parts.

TOM: You *are* the good part.

CHARLOTTE: More than me! We've been in a dark hole—

TOM: The hole of moral responsibility?

CHARLOTTE: Whatever. Imprisoned by some infinite glance backwards as if it's only the past that matters.

TOM: [*sardonic*] Well … it's a reasonably gripping narrative.

CHARLOTTE: Germany is more than an infinite well of moral culpability—A cinnamon bun would argue this much more effectively—

TOM: Is this where we break into the national anthem?

CHARLOTTE: You know the first time I ever heard the German anthem sung collectively was before the World Cup in 2006?

TOM: What a wonderful moment.

This is still all banter. She pours water in a French press.

CHARLOTTE: There's a collective psychosis that's shaped the entire political mess that Germany's in. Merkel's opening of the borders … She wanted to show the world we're the good guys but no-one talks about the complications.

TOM: What complications?

She pours.

CHARLOTTE: The majority we've let in are male and Middle Eastern who think women should be barefoot and pregnant and gays should be hurled off the top of buildings.

TOM: I can see now where you might bond with your neighbour.

CHARLOTTE: Of course we have to show compassion. But we can't be dishonest about the reality. No-one wants the Turks, not the Right obviously, but not the Left either, if they're honest, which they aren't. There are things happening here and now that demand our full attention. The Far Right is the third largest political party in the country. Hate crimes are on the increase.

We're economically in bed with Iran when wc should be sanctioning those fuckers. Every time we walk out of our door, we are hijacked by the past and can't find anything to exult in. The country is suffocating in its history …

TOM: Well, that's the price. Isn't it?

CHARLOTTE: Is it?

TOM: We can stand on the pavement down there on *Oderberg Strasse* and see—very clearly—that family dragged out of their apartment and taken away to the trains. It's right in front of us.

She's perturbed but not offended.

CHARLOTTE: Shit, Tom … That's weird.

TOM: Is that why Berlin is such a party town? Because it needs to continuously distract itself from that 'infinite well of moral culpability'?

CHARLOTTE: No. It's because it's fun and until recently, it was cheap. And young people congregate in places that are fun and cheap. And young people hold the world in the palm of their hands because everyone wants what we've got.

TOM: The crowds at the clubs are dancing or getting drug-fucked out of … self-preservation.

CHARLOTTE: Self-preservation?

TOM: Frightened their past will sabotage their future and I get it—this city runs on an engine of desperation—you can feel it—

CHARLOTTE: You've only been here three days!

TOM: This population of hipsters hell-bent on sex and art, this adrenaline built on the desperate need to grow something out of the ashes.

CHARLOTTE: The ashes? The war was seventy-five years ago.

TOM: Aren't we just trying to make so much noise it drowns out—

He stops.

CHARLOTTE: What?

TOM: You know what.

Beat. She looks at him, quizzically.

The … screams.

Beat. What did he say?

CHARLOTTE: The screams?

Beat. She's shocked: where did this come from?

From the … gas chambers? … That's a really fucking awful thing to say.

He moves towards her, conciliatory, but she moves back, away.

And I think it's fine we go to bars and get shit-faced and fuck and … and … drown out the screams. *Actually*.

He absorbs this.

The planet is literally burning to death or drowning to death … Those polar bears in Hudson Bay are dying … Looking back is an indulgence. It's an act of poetry.

TOM: You like poetry.

CHARLOTTE: But we need to be pragmatic.

TOM: Never a good word for a German.

CHARLOTTE: Don't suggest I'm unmoved! But we have to move on. Because grief is incapacitating us. We have to believe in ourselves again to make things happen.

TOM: Who or what is Germany grieving for?

CHARLOTTE: [*momentarily stumped*] … Everything. When we come out of the *U-bahn* to buy chocolate at *Kadewe* and see the sign 'From this station were deported the victims of the holocaust to *Treblinka*, to *Auschwitz*, to *Bergen-Belsen* … ' You think we walk past, bored, unseeing? We're in a stranglehold.

TOM: You sound like a victim.

CHARLOTTE: *Everyone's* a victim in war. [*Beat. She's shocked.*] Fuck, Tom … I walk across *Babbelplatz* every day and think about the students who burnt the books. That's more shocking to me than the gas chambers. Every day there's a little pause in my brain like it has to catch up to itself. I wish I could *not* think of that. Because I think I'd be a better person if I could move on. If I belonged to *right now*.

TOM: But *right now* … is what it is … *because* of then. You wouldn't be a better person if you could 'move on', Charlotte.

CHARLOTTE: I'm only—You're twisting—I'm saying there are people who suffer *now*. *Right now*. Who don't have voices. And their voices deserve to be heard but we're distracted by the past and they are … drowned out by …

TOM: By?

CHARLOTTE: Well …

TOM: Say it.

CHARLOTTE: This is silly. Why are we talking about this?

TOM: *Say* it.

CHARLOTTE: Your screams. Your screams from the gas chambers.

Beat.

TOM: Charlotte …

CHARLOTTE: [*slightly defiantly*] Tom.

He looks at her. She desperately wants to go back to where they were.

I think they should be allowed to fade.

Beat. TOM, *astonished, absorbs this.* CHARLOTTE *is defiant in her silence.*

TOM: We're talking about *six million*—

CHARLOTTE: You can't draw moral comparisons, to say the holocaust was a bigger holocaust. Because if you're Syrian, it wasn't bigger.

TOM: [*quietly*] But Charlotte . It *was* bigger.

CHARLOTTE: Serbia. Rwanda. Darfur. Afghanistan. Myanmar. There are so many horrors—

TOM: Eight hundred thousand people were murdered in Rwanda.

CHARLOTTE: Is it about numbers?

TOM: Numbers matter. Of course they do.

CHARLOTTE: [*shocked*] God … I don't like—It's not useful to—

TOM: What?

CHARLOTTE: This kind of thing that has become part of the Jewish—

TOM / CHARLOTTE: Problem? / Perspective.

CHARLOTTE: I don't get what you're—

TOM: No, it's good. Say it. Say what you think.

CHARLOTTE: Whatever I say … You seem to want to misinterpret.

TOM: Try me.

CHARLOTTE: A kind of … 'over-possessiveness'.

Beat.

TOM: Over-possessiveness?

CHARLOTTE: You *know* what I mean.

Beat.

TOM: Of?

CHARLOTTE: Suffering.

It's a strange and terrible moment: this argument appearing out of the beautiful, interesting night. She has to explain! He has to realise!

Shit. Forget it.

TOM: *No*.

She rises to the challenge.

CHARLOTTE: Say we're the last two people on Earth.

TOM: We *are* the last two people on Earth.

CHARLOTTE: A German and a Jew. Three quarters of a century later. Don't we owe it to—the future no less than the past, to speak honestly about what we feel?

TOM: Yes.

CHARLOTTE: Okay, so—

TOM: But you'll forgive me my vigilance. As you said, 'the Far Right is the third largest party in Germany'. Isn't 'moral culpability' kind of important?

CHARLOTTE: We can't fix that with shame. Holding onto the past isn't going to stop people looking for easy answers now. People want easier lives.

TOM: It can't hurt to remind them—

CHARLOTTE: [*On a roll*] And for very respectful reasons, it's hard for people to see Jews as victims.

Beat.

TOM: [*neutral*] Right.

CHARLOTTE: You're so *good* at surviving.

He looks at her, shocked.

Listen, young Germans are best-practice empathisers. Guilt flowed in our mother's milk. The millions of ordinary Germans who averted their gaze … Accountants and lawyers, soldiers, plumbers, bakers … they turned away from *their own moment*. They chose not to see what was going on. We can't make the same mistake. We have to draw a line. We need to be *here*.

TOM *looks out of the window, silent.*

What are we doing?

TOM: I don't know.

CHARLOTTE: This is just—Let's go back to bed. I don't know how we got onto this. This is crazy! This whole thing. I've always identified with the Jews!

TOM: Absolutely.

CHARLOTTE: [*coldly*] What are you doing?

Beat.

TOM: You think we should 'draw a line'.

So it's not over.

CHARLOTTE: I respect the past! As much as you do. I just don't think Europe should be forever a graveyard.

TOM: *But it is.*

CHARLOTTE: An endlessly articulated collective memory? I don't think that's about honouring anything.

TOM: So, why?

CHARLOTTE: Why?

TOM: Why do we insist on remembering?

CHARLOTTE: Well as every primary student can tell you, so that history never repeats. I get that.

TOM: Okay.

CHARLOTTE: *And—*

TOM: And—

CHARLOTTE: Because it's a way of—

TOM: What?

CHARLOTTE: A way of being permanently—

TOM: Permanently?

CHARLOTTE: I don't know!

TOM: Say it!

CHARLOTTE: Let's stop this.

TOM: Permanently what?

CHARLOTTE: Permanently—

TOM: What?!

CHARLOTTE: … Special.

Long beat as he takes this in.

Don't make me out to be—I'm more admiring of the Jews than—

TOM: Hey, was that why you 'waved uncertainly' as I was crossing the street, drunk? Outside the club?

CHARLOTTE: [*confused*] What?

TOM: So you could save your own special Jew?

CHARLOTTE: [*shocked*] 'My own Jew'? You're … crazy! I didn't even know you were Jewish!

TOM: Didn't my air of 'intellectual intensity' give it away?

CHARLOTTE: [*ignoring the dig*] I'm talking about mercy. Show some mercy.

TOM: You want to draw a universal finish line? On remembering? Well … I don't think you should ever forget.

CHARLOTTE: Okay … [*Defiantly*] Maybe *we* shouldn't. But maybe *you* should. [*Beat.*] At some point the tallying has to be over. No more math over what is owed and who owes and who is owed. Isn't that what we want—all of us?

A coldness has come between them. She's mystified about how this whole thing has got to here.

What are you doing? Tom … this is weird. I don't get it. I'm—this night was—I thought—Fuck. Weren't we—weren't we—falling? Am I wrong? I think I was—I was! I was falling …

He's wracked ... angry but so powerfully connected to her.

TOM: It's okay. It's okay to say these things.

He walks over to kiss her but she moves away. He's shaken. What's going on? What does he want? What has he found? What might he lose?

CHARLOTTE: You meet a girl in a bar in Berlin. You have great—I think—Am I wrong? Maybe it could—who knows? … I feel as if I've known you forever. It might … It mightn't but it might … *Become* something. Am I crazy?

TOM: It *is* something.

CHARLOTTE: But you're trying to push me into a corner and I don't know why. I don't think we disagree. I think we're … bizarrely in tune. And I also … I also feel as if you … As if this night has been … I've never fallen so …

TOM: Fallen so—

Suddenly the hard buzz of the intercom front door buzzer. A moment as they take this in.

Don't answer.

She's surprised by this.

[*Very seriously*] Don't answer that.

CHARLOTTE: Why?

TOM: It's probably your neighbour.

CHARLOTTE: He's a shift worker. He's sleeping.

The buzzer goes again. TOM *walks over to the intercom on the wall and answers it.*

TOM: Fuck off.

She looks at him, confused.

CHARLOTTE: What's going on?

TOM: What's going on is that I'm really fucking into you.

The buzzer goes again. TOM *again speaks into the intercom.*

I SAID: FUCK OFF. GO AWAY. GET LOST.

CHARLOTTE: What are you doing?

TOM: I'm telling them to fuck off is what I'm doing.

CHARLOTTE: What's wrong with you? Why are you being so weird?

Silence. They stare at one another.

Before. When you said all that about leaving. About Portugal. About Samoa. You said something.

TOM: I said: 'Let's go.' I said 'that I was falling into something'—I was—I want to be with you.

CHARLOTTE: 'Let's leave this apartment', you said. My ex-boyfriend. My mother's cat sculpture. Remember? Leave it all behind, you said.

TOM: I meant it.

CHARLOTTE: 'Let's leave the painting and your great-grandfather and Berlin.'

Beat.

Why did you say that?

TOM: [*quickly*] I'm saying: We will start again.

CHARLOTTE: My 'great-grandfather'? Why not my 'grandfather'? Why not my 'family'?

TOM: I meant your family. Of course that's what I meant.

CHARLOTTE: But you said: 'my *great*-grandfather'. I've been wondering about it all night.

The buzzer again. TOM *walks over to it and pulls the wired buzzer aggressively out of the wall and throws it on the floor. It could be frustration or possibly ... something more dangerous. She's paralysed with fear.*

TOM *composes himself.*

TOM: Constable was actually very cutting edge. Everyone else was doing ruins. But he just looked at what was in front of him. A wild

wild sea. The storm clouds. The majesty and terror of the inner world, given to nature.

She looks at him, very surprised.

CHARLOTTE: So, you *do* know Constable?

TOM: It's not a reproduction.

Beat. CHARLOTTE *ponders, confused.*

CHARLOTTE: [*uncertain where this is going*] Okay. It's not a reproduction.

Beat.

TOM: Two point five … Two point eight … million. Conservatively.

Beat.

Why did you lie about that?

CHARLOTTE: What?

TOM: Why did you say it was a reproduction?

CHARLOTTE: [*off guard, off balance*] I tell everyone that because I can't afford to insure it …

TOM: You underestimated me.

CHARLOTTE: Okay. So? You know it's real. I hardly know you. I met you in a bar *yesterday*. I told you it was a reproduction because that's what I say.

TOM: The vivid light and colour. Broken brushstrokes. Expressionistic energy. The romance of the storm with the light attempting to peek through: a window to the sublime. The sky was the whole point for him, wasn't it?

She's trying to work out what this is about.

CHARLOTTE: Do you judge me for being rich? Is that it?

TOM: It's a beautiful painting.

CHARLOTTE: My mother transferred ownership to me so it didn't become part of the divorce settlement.

TOM: I doubt your great-grandfather, the art collector Wolfgang Schmidt, ever imagined it would end up in a student's loft in *Prenzlauer Berg*.

Beat. Her mind is working overtime to put it all together. She begins to realise …

CHARLOTTE: [*quietly, the start of fear*] Who are you?
TOM: I'm who I said I was.
CHARLOTTE: Are you a collector?
TOM: No.

He's clearly dangerous. How dangerous?

CHARLOTTE: What are you doing here?
TOM: I came for the painting.

She looks confused.

CHARLOTTE: What?
TOM: Yes.

She smiles. This can't be serious.

CHARLOTTE: [*quiet incredulity*] You want my painting?
TOM: I want *my* painting.

Beat.

As TOM *speaks, a trembling* CHARLOTTE *takes a step back. Visible to the audience, but not to* TOM, *she uses her hands behind her to pick up the kitchen knife she'd left on the kitchen bench earlier, and holds it behind her back.*

TOM: The house on *Drakestrasse*. The house that is now an architect's office, once full of art and books—had in its dining room a very special painting that my great-grandfather had purchased as a gift for my great-grandmother.

Their eyes meet. CHARLOTTE, *disbelieving, continues to listen, profoundly shocked.*

The Nazis forced the sale of his collection for a few *deutchmarks*, intent on building acquisitions for Hitler's *Führermuseum* … The sale was handled by an intermediary for the Nazis. An art-dealer who strong-armed Jules into relinquishing his art, including a very valuable, if slightly overbearing, Constable … The art dealer was Wolfgang Schmidt.

Beat.

CHARLOTTE: [*shocked*] What?

Beat.

TOM: And surveying the collection with a professional's eye, Wolfgang Schmidt kept one for himself. A seascape with a stormy sky …

TOM *and* CHARLOTTE *both turn slowly to look at the Constable.*

CHARLOTTE: You came to the bar … knowing who I was?

Beat.

And then you chatted me up?

Beat.

You knew I'd follow you out? And invite you back here …

Beat.

[*Incredulous*] And then you fucked me?

TOM: Not part of the plan.

CHARLOTTE: The plan?

CHARLOTTE, *suddenly filled with rage, launches herself at* TOM *with the knife. To avoid it, he goes flying back.*

His lip is bleeding. He lies on the floor, in pain, shocked too. Nobody moves.

After a while, he sits up.

TOM: My mother has photographs of the house on *Drakestrasse*. The Constable is there above a pretty Biedemeier side table. There are Cubist works by Klee, a small Picasso drawing and a Chagall.

In Jules' study is the most beautiful of all, a small antiquity, Aphrodite … white as snow … and preternaturally serene …

CHARLOTTE *listens in shocked silence.*

I wasn't interested at first. I didn't want to get drawn into … I don't know. But my mother showed me the databases … It was just a—a casual thing—but the pieces started to come together … The Nazis meticulously documented what they stole. Over 20,000 works on neatly typed index cards, now online. I found the Picasso and the Chagall and the Klee. But no Constable. No Aphrodite. I went back through the records to see how the works were acquired … And I began to wonder if the dealer hadn't kept a memento for himself. Lo and behold, the Constable was formally listed when your parents put it into the Sotheby's sale in '89. They retracted it, as you know. [*Beat.*] Perhaps they knew someone might be looking for it.

Beat. He allows a moment for this to sink in.

It wasn't hard to track your mother via her own website. I told her I was writing my doctorate on English Romantic painters and I'd love to see her Constable. 'My daughter Charlotte has it,' she said. 'In Berlin.' Your Facebook page had enough clues to narrow it down. Shots of you hanging out of a window in summer above a ramen place, et cetera. There's a photo of you on your street in a crazy wig with your street number behind you. Your neighbour was kind enough to tell me you were working at the bar when I bumped into him on the stairwell. [*Beat.*] And there you were. [*Beat.*] And here I am.

CHARLOTTE: [*explosive*] Get the fuck out of here!

TOM: I can't leave without the painting.

CHARLOTTE: It's not your painting!

TOM: Charlotte …

CHARLOTTE: Get out of here!

Distraught, shocked, she picks up the packet of cigarettes, calming herself, taking a moment to absorb, lights it, draws on it.

You want me to give you the painting? Because eighty years ago your great-grandfather sold it cheaply to my great-grandfather?

TOM: 'You can be responsible for something you're not actually guilty of.'

He points to the window.

Look out there and tell me honestly you can't see the Rosens being taken away? The street's exactly the fucking same, Charlotte! But for the Aesop shop. And the fucking pour-over coffee shop that sells 200 euro trainers? Eighty years is nothing.

CHARLOTTE: My great-grandfather was probably given no choice! The Nazis had him over a barrel …

TOM: Who knows?

CHARLOTTE: Of course they did!

TOM: Okay … so circumstances lead him there. But *somehow* he ended up with a Constable that belonged to a Jew in *Drakestrasse*. And when the war ended, he didn't try to find the Jew.

CHARLOTTE: If our situation was reversed, would you give it to me?

TOM: We'll never know. *Because I'm the Jew and you're the German.*

They stare at each other. CHARLOTTE *walks over to the painting and stands in front of it,* TOM *watching. Long beat. The fury quietened ...*

CHARLOTTE: Imagine if he knew, Constable, if he had a premonition. Between him and us, industrialisation, two world wars, the space age, the internet. And now his beloved sky carrying catastrophic change to the planet … How simple it was for him. For the sky to just be the sky. For a painting to just be a painting.

She turns to TOM.

You *hunted* me. You *spied* on me.

TOM: That was before—before I saw you, met you, fucked you, knew you—

CHARLOTTE: You mean, *yesterday*? … The sad thing is—I'm on your side, Tom.

Beat.

TOM: 'Our' side?

CHARLOTTE: The holocaust was a crime against all humanity. But it wasn't German. It was *human*. You judge but can you possibly know what it was—

TOM: [*interrupting*] We judge the man who hit your brother chasing the ball. And we judge the woman who picked me and Adam up and hit a tree and killed him. There were a thousand reasons she drove fast. But there was the moment she denied herself the chance to resist. There is always a choice. I know it's not your fault, Charlotte. Of course I know that! *But not everyone would have shoved humans into ovens.*

CHARLOTTE: [*distraught*] You need to be a real fucking Jew.

TOM: Be a real Jew?

CHARLOTTE: Don't be a Jew when someone makes a crass joke. Be a *real* Jew. Isn't it about beauty and expansiveness and *life*? My parents never wanted me to hold their grief for Daniel in my palm and clench it. Your great-grandfather on *Drakestrasse* didn't want that for you.

TOM: It's not the same.

CHARLOTTE: You make glib comments about faith as part of your flirtation routine. You grab hold of a historical period and pin it to your jacket lapel, refusing to let go. You use it as a moral embellishment and turn *Auschwitz* into a spectacle. You're forcing those people to die over and over again. You can't earn your distinction by claiming their experience! That's not honouring them. If you want to honour them, *live*. 'Let life happen to you. Life is in the right always.'

TOM: One day you'll be sixty. You'll be in a park playing with your grandkid … And it will suddenly come to you that you're the sum total of what came before you. You had one chance. This. Now.

CHARLOTTE: No. *You'll* be sixty. Sitting alone in your bedsit with your piles of hoarded newspapers blocking the light and the sound of other people's children playing in the playground outside, the children of the children you never had because you didn't know how to go with the present, how to run with it, run with someone headlong into something and it will suddenly come to you that you're the sum total of what came before *you* and *you* had one chance. This. Now.

Beat.

Justice isn't a painting. It's us.

Beat.

TOM: Okay.

CHARLOTTE: Okay?

TOM: Okay. You win. Let's make it start again. I told you that. That's what I want! We start again. The clock. *From now.* And *we* will be justice.

CHARLOTTE: [*incredulously*] You think we can start again *now*?

TOM: [*fighting for his life*] Tell me you don't … Say it. Say you don't feel—

TOM *walks over to her and stands very close to her, looking her straight in the eyes. Suddenly he leans in and kisses her.*

She bends into him, just as passionate, just as wanting and then suddenly, disgusted by herself, she pulls away, backs away. She stares at him, distraught.

CHARLOTTE: You are … my *stolpersteine*.

Beat.

Suddenly she runs to the painting, to take it from the wall. He reacts as if her removing it will kill him. As if he'll lose everything that matters.

TOM: I don't want it!

She lifts it off.

CHARLOTTE: You're playing games!
TOM: I'm serious!
CHARLOTTE: Your brother might have something to say about that!
TOM: I'll tell him it turned out to be a fake!
CHARLOTTE: You'd lie?
TOM: Yes.
CHARLOTTE: [*hard, resolute*] Take it!
TOM: Keep it!
CHARLOTTE: I won't!

She rests the painting on the floor and pushes the top so that it could easily fall. He has to leap forward to catch it. He holds it but he doesn't want it.

TOM: [*pleading*] Charlotte … I swear. It's over.

Beat.

CHARLOTTE: It's *never* going to be over.

He's devastated, utterly torn.

They're both spent, exhausted, ruined.

A long beat.

A shaken, ambivalent TOM *walks towards the door, carrying the painting, looks at her, then leaves, closing the door behind him.*

She's alone and her aloneness feels suddenly palpable.

She looks at the space where the painting hung. Dawn is breaking through the window, light gently coming up and flooding the loft, inch by inch.

She looks across at the trunk/coffee table, kneels behind it and lifts the lid. Carefully, she removes a small wrapped object.

She unwraps the fabric to reveal a gleaming white classical sculpture. Aphrodite.

She goes to the mantlepiece and sits the bust upon it, a small object compared to the last one.

She steps back to take it in.

The sunlight from the window strikes it. It's golden, suffused by sun. She studies it. The beauty of it.

The lights start to dim.

Suddenly, she jumps up and races to the window and lifts it up.

CHARLOTTE: [*yelling*] Tom! Tom!

She looks back at Aphrodite, then back through the window:

[*Yelling*] Tom! Tom! Tom!

Black out.

THE END

Other plays by Joanna Murray-Smith and available from Currency Press

HONOUR

What happens when everything you have used to define yourself—every quality, role and affiliation—suddenly abandon you? What happens when a mature, intelligent, responsible and loving woman finds her life disappearing?

ISBN 978 0 86819 782 1

LOVE CHILD

A reconciliation between a mother and the daughter she gave away at birth. Anna defines herself through her political conscience and she believes she has come to terms with her history until a young woman arrives at her door.

ISBN 978 0 86819 546 9

NIGHTFALL

It's twilight, and a mother and father wait for the promised return of their daughter who vanished ten years earlier. A stranger arrives at their doorstep, warning them that their daughter will only return on certain agonising terms.

ISBN 978 0 86819 919 1

RAPTURE

A vivid play set among intelligent and educated people whose cynicism appears to answer all questions and who navigate uncertainty with ease. What could possibly shock or unsettle them? When two of their number claim to have found God, the consequences are profound. Ethics and certainties are tested on a battleground of inexplicable belief.

ISBN 978 0 86819 679 4

BOMBSHELLS

Six monologues made famous by actress Caroline O'Connor, exposing six women balancing their inner and outer lives with humour and often desperate cunning. They range in age from a feisty teenager to a 64-year-old widow yearning for the unexpected.

ISBN 978 0 86819 751 7

THE FEMALE OF THE SPECIES

Thirty years ago Margot Mason, pioneer of the 1970s Women's Liberation movement and fearless academic, wrote her groundbreaking work. Now she is faced with Molly, an unannounced visitor who produces a gun and calmly informs Margot that she intends to kill her because she blames her for warping her mother's mind and ruining her life with her hit book *The Cerebral Vagina*.

ISBN 978 0 86819 825 5

NINETY

It is no use, but William gives Isobel ninety minutes anyway. They were once married—and now Isabel just wants ninety minutes. Soon William will be married again, so ninety is all she has to make her case. Ninety to remember what they had. Ninety to regain what was lost. Just ninety minutes to rediscover love or call it a day, forever.

ISBN 978 0 86819 851 4

ROCKABYE

Sidney can feel her career slipping down the plughole. No-one loves a pop star when she's forty—not if she isn't Madonna or Kylie. So unless she wants to join the ranks of the has-beens on the casino circuit, she'd better get herself a hit. But what if she regains the whole world and still feels that something's missing?

ISBN 978 0 86819 860 6

SONGS FOR NOBODIES

When a great singer lets her voice float out over the anonymous crowd, or form the grooves of thousands of records, or flow through radios into millions of homes across the world, she makes countless unknown connections with people. In *Songs for Nobodies*, we meet five unknown women who are touched by the great singers seen to be living the dream: Judy Garland, Patsy Cline, Edith Piaf, Billie Holiday and Maria Callas. Five great singers, five monologues.

ISBN 978 0 86819 893 4

THE GIFT

Sadie and Ed meet Martin and Chloë at a holiday resort and instantly hit it off, despite coming from completely different worlds. When Martin saves Ed's life, everyone knows the debt can never be properly repaid. But Ed is rich and Chloë and Martin have a need so great it seems divine providence when Ed, wanting to show his gratitude, gives the young couple a year to decide on an appropriate gift. Yet when the year is up, surely Chloë and Martin's wish is something no-one could possibly grant?

ISBN 978 0 86819 915 3

STORIES OF LOVE AND DECEPTION

An anthology of three plays, *Stories of Love and Deception* is a keenly engaging discussion of our most dearly-held values and their ramifications. This trilogy includes *Day One, a Hotel, Evening*; *True Minds*; and *Fury*.

ISBN 978 1 92500 530 1